TE

MASON, P.

Textiles

70002946711   Pbk

Please return/renew this item by the last date shown

worcestershire
c o u n t y c o u n c i l
Cultural Services

Directions In Art

Textiles

Paul Mason

www.heinemann.co.uk/library
Visit our website to find out more inform

To order:
☎ Phone 44 (0) 1865 888066
🖹 Send a fax to 44 (0) 1865 314091
💻 Visit the Heinemann Bookshop at www.h catalogue and order online.

First published in Great Britain by Heinemann Library, Halley Court, Jordan Hill, Oxford OX2 8EJ, part of Harcourt Education.
Heinemann is a registered trademark of Harcourt Education Ltd.

Editorial: Lucy Thunder and Helen Cannons
Design: Jo Hinton-Malivoire and AMR
Picture Research: Hannah Taylor and Elaine Willis
Production: Edward Moore

Originated by Ambassador Litho Ltd
Printed and bound in China by South China Printing Company

ISBN 0 431 17644 2 (hardback)
07 06 05
10 9 8 7 6 5 4 3 2

ISBN 0 431 17654 X (paperback)
08 07 06 05 04
10 9 8 7 6 5 4 3 2 1

British Library Cataloguing in Publication Data
Mason, Paul
Textiles. – (Directions in art)
746
A full catalogue record for this book is available from the British Library.

Acknowledgements
The Publishers would like to thank the following for permission to reproduce photographs: Michael Brennand-Wood pp**9**, **10**; Bridgeman Art Library / National Gallery, London p**45**; Penny Burnfield / Photoshades p**13 top**; Penny Burnfield / Paul Mason p**13 bottom**; Penny Burnfield / Garrick Palmer p**14**; Becky Early pp**18 bottom**, **18 top**; Becky Early p**19**; Jo Gordon / Paul Mason p**21**; Jo Gordon / Ed Barber / Crafts Council Photostore p**22**; Rachael Howard pp**25**, **26**; Rachael Howard / Paul Mason p**27**; Hikaru Noguchi / Nick Turner / The Crafts Council Photostore p**29**; Jessica Ogden p**31**; Vauthey Pierre / Corbis Sygma p**6**; Fran Reed 1999 p**32**; Fran Reed 2002 p**33**; Fran Reed 2000 p**35**; Sophie Roet p**5**; Sophie Roet/Lon Van Kenlen p**36**; Sophie Roet/Marcus Ginns p**38**; Norman Sherfield pp**40**, **41**, **42**; Yinka Shonibare / Courtesy Stephen Friedman Gallery, London, Collection National Gallery of Canada p**44**; Yinka Shonibare/ Courtesy Stephen Friedman Gallery p**47**; Georgina von Etzdorf/ Paul Mason pp**48**, **49**.
Cover photograph of *Water Fabric* by Sophie Roet reproduced with permission of Sophie Roet.

The Publishers would like to thank Richard Stemp, Gallery Educator at the Tate, London, for his assistance in the preparation of this book.

CONTENTS

Any words appearing in the text in bold, **like this**, are explained in the Glossary.

DIRECTIONS IN TEXTILES

Of all art forms, textiles may be one of the most varied. Someone who says they are a 'textiles artist' might mean a lot of different things. They might create sculptural shapes using knots, like Norman Sherfield (see pages 40–43). They could specialize in making basket-sculptures from the skins of fish, like Fran Reed (see pages 32–35). They might use textiles as an important part of a bigger project, like the African-inspired cloths used by Yinka Shonibare (see pages 44–47). Or they might use a variety of different techniques and materials to create assemblages of pieces, like Penny Burnfield's (see pages 12–15).

All this variety might make you ask, 'What are textiles?' The ordinary dictionary gives a very simple definition of the word 'textile': '1 any woven material. 2 any cloth.' So textile art must be art using either woven material or cloth, then? Well, yes... and no. Fran Reed's baskets aren't made of woven material or cloth; they're made of fish skins; Norman Sherfield's works are made of different kinds of thread. We need to look deeper to try to reach an understanding of what textile art and design is.

Changing textiles

The use of textiles in fine art is fairly recent. Until the 20th century, textiles were mainly practical. Felting, weaving, knitting and so on produced things people could use, such as fabric for hats and sweaters. Some of these textiles were very beautiful, skilled pieces of work – complicated **couture** dresses, or intricate wallpaper designs, for example. But they would have been unlikely to appear in museums and galleries in the same way as paintings.

Now, many fine artists use elements of textiles technique in their work. Textiles have moved from the drawing room to the art gallery.

Textiles techniques

Textiles artists and designers have a huge variety of techniques available to them. Many people combine more than one of these in a piece of work. Imagine a piece of art using several different techniques. First the actual fabric may have to be created. This could involve **weaving**, **knitting**, crochet or **felting** in order to make traditional fabrics. Other artists use more imaginative and unusual basic materials – fish skins, paper or animal gut, for example.

Once the basic fabric has been created, there are still plenty of things an artist might do with it before their work is finished. They may print on it in some way, using **screen-printing** or **heat transfer** printing for example. They could also paint it in a variety of ways, stitch it, embroider it, bond (join) it to another fabric, or add a skeleton to give it shape.

Textiles in two parts

Some of the people featured in this book are usually concerned mainly with the textile itself. Sophie Roet (see pages 36–39), for example, has created fascinating, innovative textiles that are used by fashion designers but also appear in international exhibitions. One of Becky Early's (see pages 16–19) heat-transfer designs was used in hospital gowns; another was worn to an awards ceremony by the singer, Björk.

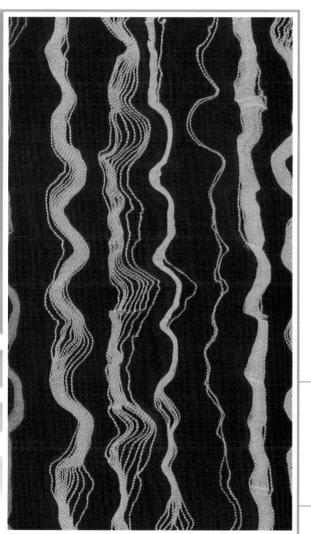

Other artists and designers are concerned not just with the textile itself but also with what is created from it. Yinka Shonibare's African fabric paintings were developed into part of a **multi-faceted** body of work that was shown in art galleries as the 'Dressing Down' exhibition. The ideas used by Georgina von Etzdorf (see pages 48–49) may once have inspired art exhibitions, but they still end up on the shelves of exclusive stores around the world, to be bought as scarves.

Fabrics, like Wandering Lines *by Sophie Roet, are as likely to appear in galleries as on the catwalk.*

Some textile artists use apparently ordinary fabrics, but turn them into something more through imagination and technique. Rachael Howard (see pages 24–27), for example, was driven by her love of sketching to develop a unique method of working. One reviewer said that Howard's work pioneered 'a lively mix of embroidery and screen-printing techniques that owes as much to *The Beano* as academia.' Such work – not just Howard's, but that of other artists, too – is sometimes difficult for traditionalists to accept as art.

Scarves, like these on the catwalk, can be inspired by original pieces of textile art.

But is it art?

Textiles artists have not always been accepted as full members of the art world. The Penguin *Dictionary of Art and Artists*, for example, has no entry under 'textiles' – though it has plenty to say about sculpture.

The crossover between textile art and design and fashion makes it difficult sometimes to say where one ends and the other begins. Some textile artists and designers are more at the fashion end of the spectrum – Hikaru Noguchi, for example, came up with her unique patterns and techniques in a commercial context, designing knitwear. Most of the people working in or with the fashion industry have a strong background in art. Jo Gordon, whose **felt** hairstyle hats are discussed on pages 20–24, studied Sculpture before going on to the Royal College of Art. But the work of textile artists can often be **mass-produced** in a way that doesn't fit well with the traditional idea of 'art'.

Other textiles artists and designers wouldn't imagine that they would ever see their work used in a fashion show. Fran Reed's basket-sculptures, or Norman Sherfield's knotted shapes, are one-off pieces, intensely personal to the artist and impossible for anyone else to reproduce.

Today there are plenty of exciting and interesting things going on in the world of textiles. The artists and designers in this book represent a wide variety of different kinds of work, using materials that range from fish skins to something not unlike kitchen foil. Some are closely linked to the world of fine art; others are more interested in making a living through high fashion. From the art gallery to the catwalk, textiles have something to offer almost everyone!

Pop goes the art debate!

During the late 1950s and 1960s, an art movement call Pop Art began to attract a lot of attention. Pop Art used everyday objects – beef burgers, tins of tuna fish, flags – as its subjects. When people began to ask if such mundane things could really be art, some of the Pop Artists responded by making art that could be mass-produced. Andy Warhol (1926–87), one of the leading figures in the Pop Art movement, named his new studio 'The Factory' and churned out hundreds of prints of each piece, in an effort to undermine the traditional idea of what was meant by 'art'.

MICHAEL BRENNAND-WOOD

Michael Brennand-Wood is one of the most respected textile artists working today. He is also one of the most controversial. A visitor to the 1995 *Art of the Stitch* exhibition was overheard saying that his work was 'more art than stitch'. Brennand-Wood's work blurs the line between textiles work and fine art.

Bury in Lancashire, UK, where Brennand-Wood was born in 1952, was once at the heart of England's cotton industry. His grandmother had worked as a weaver at one of the local mills. She taught her grandson how to knit and sew, and he remembers cupboards full of **calico** and bed linen in her house. These very same pieces of cloth ended up being used in his work many years later.

Another childhood influence on Brennand-Wood was his grandfather, a keen engineer. They worked together on various projects, making almost anything from metal or wood. These two childhood experiences became an integral part of Brennand-Wood's later work as an artist.

Brennand-Wood knew early on that he wanted to be an artist. When he left school at sixteen he went straight to Bolton College of Art to do a Foundation course, before starting a Textiles degree at Manchester Polytechnic, then an MA in Textiles at Birmingham University. Almost immediately after leaving university he began to achieve success in the art world, and now, over twenty years later, his work is known around the world. He has exhibited in Europe, Japan, Australia and elsewhere, and has been shortlisted for a wide range of awards.

Themes and influences

One of the key themes of Brennand-Wood's art is the three-dimensional features of cloth itself. The **warp** and **weft** threads of a woven fabric, different styles of stitching, and the patterns and shapes of fabrics from around the world all appear as ideas in his art.

Further inspiration comes from maps and charts. The strong circular shapes of his pieces *Navigator* or *Diviner*, for example, recall the style of early maps of the world, or Buddhist maps of the different stages of life. Some of Brennand-Wood's earlier works are based on wooden frameworks. These were actually inspired by the warp and weft threads of cloth, but in some pieces – *Broken English*, for example – the 'grid' made by the framework also stirs an echo of the gridlines of a map or a piece of graph paper.

Brennand-Wood has also used photography as a starting point for pieces of work. Microscopic photos of the structure of cells, for example, inspire elements of some pieces, as do aerial photos of African villages.

Diviner *(1990) is a piece made with inlaid wood, fabric collage, wax and acrylic.*

Music is another key part of the process of producing art. Brennand-Wood is a follower of experimental musicians such as Philip Glass and John Cage. He says 'I am always listening to a piece of music while I work.' John Cage's idea that chance has an important part to play in an artist's creative process is reflected in Brennand-Wood's work.

Another theme is the use of early forms of writing, which often consisted of drawings or **symbols** rather than the letters we use today. At one time Brennand-Wood studied this, looking for 'connections between drawing systems and stitchery: stitch as **notation**.'

Finally, inspiration comes from other cultures: the repeated patterns of Asian carpets, the styles of central Asian **embroidery**, **felt** making and other non-European textiles all feed into Brennand-Wood's work in various ways.

You Are Here

You Are Here is the title of a major piece finished in 1997, which was shortlisted for the Jerwood Prize for Applied Arts: Textiles in that same year. The title immediately reminds people of the maps that are dotted around all over the place: in city centres, railway stations and motorway service stations. *You Are Here* does reflect Brennand-Wood's interest in maps and charts of various sorts, but also stands as the artist's statement to himself. *You Are Here* is a piece of work where Brennand-Wood is saying to himself 'this is where I've got to.'

> You Are Here ... *is both a cultural and personal map, a good place for those arriving at Brennand-Wood's work for the first time. The work summarizes Brennand-Wood's development as an artist, offering a tour of twenty years of research, experimenting, imagining. This is a work about taking stock at the mid point of both a life and a career.*
> PAMELA JOHNSON, IN *MICHAEL BRENNAND-WOOD*, 1999.

Technique and design

You Are Here is made of wood, into which grooves or routes have been carved. These have been inlaid with cloth. Brennand-Wood devised this technique in order to create a layering system, implying a sense of something waiting to be discovered. 'In one sense,' he says, 'the work is a personal Internet of ideas. The red cloth symbolizes blood, capillaries of energy and information moving back and forth.' Dotted across the piece are tiny electric bulbs, providing random illuminations. Again the viewer is reminded of the maps that stand around city centres, using electric bulbs to show where you are standing or key points of interest.

The markings on the far left of the piece refer to Brennand-Wood's early experiments with stitch and the 'grid' pieces. **Motifs** from Asian carpet designs are scattered about. Like Asian carpets, *You Are Here* has a design featuring a variety of centres rather than just one. Instead of being drawn to a single visual point, the viewer's eye is drawn at random from one to another and another.

Research into lace, a fabric Brennand-Wood describes as 'the encirclement, using a thread, of space', is also reflected in the piece, especially in the three circular patterns on the middle-left. The fourth circle, directly above these three, is an Aboriginal dot pattern from Australia. To the left of this is an irregular circular shape that is based on a cross-section of a piece of the Great Barrier Reef. Below and to the left of this is a prehistoric maze, with the simple shape of a man anchored in its centre.

On the bottom right is another prehistoric maze, a reflection of Brennand-Wood's interest in archaeology. Running along the bottom of *You Are Here* is something Brennand-Wood calls a 'music river', a reference to a musical score by John Cage. Cage's ideas about chance being part of the creative process are reflected in the dice rolling along the river.

The cut-out shapes of *You Are Here* provide a reminder of wood-block printing, which is used in many places as a simple way of getting a pattern on to a cloth. The required shape is carved out or cut into a flat piece of wood, which is then pressed into ink or dye and held hard against a fabric, which picks up the pattern. The same shape can be repeated again and again using this technique.

PENNY BURNFIELD

Penny Burnfield was born in South London in 1946. She went to school in Croydon, and lived near enough to London's Natural History Museum to be able to visit it regularly. At the time many of the exhibits were housed in wooden cases, with glass tops through which visitors could look. Burnfield remembers being fascinated by the simple creatures and fossils these cases contained. Decades later this fascination began to re-emerge as the inspiration for pieces of art.

When Burnfield left school she trained as a doctor. It was only 30 years later, having become interested in art through an **embroidery** evening class, that she started a degree in Textile Art at the Winchester School of Art. This, she says, was 'a struggle' because of her 'apparent inability to draw'. A breakthrough came when Burnfield realised that 'because my work is very **abstract**, the drawings also needed to be abstract'. She began to see that the **organic** shapes that appeared in these abstract drawings were linked to her interests in medicine and biology.

These organic shapes inspired many of the pieces that Burnfield is best known for today. She uses a variety of media and techniques in her work, and somehow imparts human qualities to the simple shapes she produces. Her pieces are named only once they are finished, when their characteristics have become clearer. They have been exhibited at various venues, and have brought her to international attention.

> *I look for fundamental organic forms, such as are found in simple invertebrates, seeds, pollen grains, fossils. The work also draws on archaeological artefacts from the past, the history of science and **alchemy**, and the development of writing.* PENNY BURNFIELD

I want to be Alone

This piece from 1999 (see top of page 13) combines simple shapes with human emotions in a very effective way. The left-hand figure, with its spiky tentacles sticking out, looms threateningly over its cowering neighbour. The right-hand figure seems to be trying to turn away and hide, and clearly would prefer to be alone. The piece is made using Tyvek paper (a thick, strong paper), wire and machine stitching. The shapes were created using a technique called fold braiding, using long strips of paper that had been stitched along their edges.

This picture of Burnfield's I Want to be Alone *shows the right-hand figure curling away from the other one, as if it is trying to hide.*

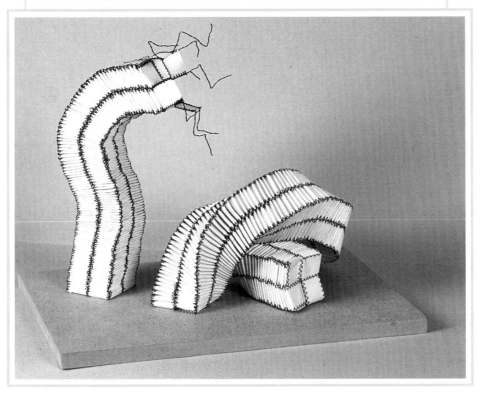

Fold braiding

The technique Burnfield used in *I Want to be Alone* is a straightforward one that can nonetheless result in very interesting shapes.

First Burnfield takes the long strip (1) and folds it down across the square of the shape (2). Then she folds the long strip from the next corner (in a clockwise direction) across the first strip (3). To complete one 'round' of folding, she tucks the strip from the next clockwise corner under the strip in front of it (4). This anchors all the sheets in place, and allows Burnfield to start the process again.

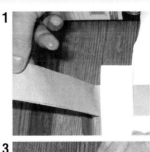

Darwin's Box

Darwin's Box (2001) is an assemblage of various pieces, which reflect the themes of Burnfield's work as well as her imaginative use of different techniques and materials. The piece is an old doctor's case filled with what look like specimens and samples that someone has collected. Poking out of one of the drawers are some old papers wrapped in ribbon. The overall impression is that the box could well be associated with the famous naturalist Charles Darwin. Darwin was a scientist whose theories about how different species developed changed the way people understood the world. He travelled far and wide while developing his ideas, and collected lots of specimens of different animals.

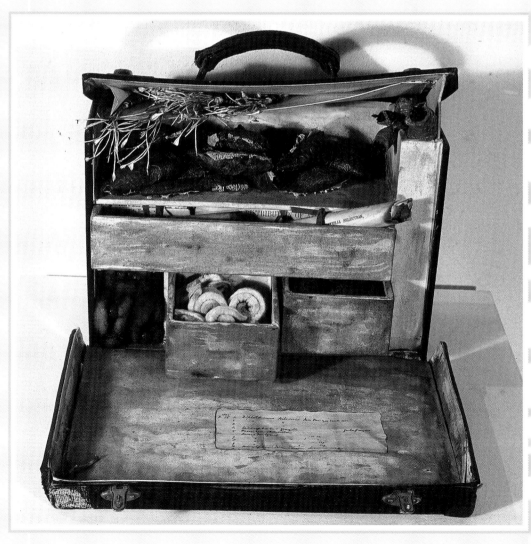

The left-behind box

The piece began with the box itself. Burnfield had an art student living in a caravan at the bottom of her garden, and the student left behind various bits and pieces when she moved on. The box was discovered later, hidden away behind the caravan, covered in ivy and Burnfield began to fill its compartments. The sections of *Darwin's Box* contain clues about the identity of the artist who created it, if those examining it know where to look and what the clues mean.

Box contents

In the very top of the box, pieces of paper string lean out like tufts of grass. Below these are **pupa**-like shapes that are actually made of dyed paper, with burned plastic peeking out of their folds. To the right are more organic shapes – these look like some sort of undersea creature, though they are made from burned paper wrapped in dyed paper and bound with thread.

The shapes in the bottom compartments are less certain. On the left are pieces made using **felt** shapes that have been dyed red and had beads and fabric added to them. The centre drawer has been pulled out to reveal more felt, as well as the first clue of the artist's identity. This time the felt has been rolled into shapes that look something like fossils. Burnfield is a keen fossil hunter, regularly visiting the beaches around Lyme Regis in Dorset in search of new ones. The contents of the right-hand drawer are hard to see – nestled inside is more felt, dyed red with rusty paint and tied with wool.

Inside the last drawer, the wide central one, is hidden the last clue. Out of the drawer pokes a paper, a cover piece from an important text on **evolution**. Inside are other papers, all also to do with evolution – all but one of them. The one, barely visible, is a part of *Doctrae Medicinae* by Linnaeus – an old medical text that serves as a reminder that Burnfield was once also a doctor.

Labels and meanings

Almost all Burnfield's pieces are labelled with scientific-looking **notations**. The labels reflect the inspiration behind the piece, and the techniques and materials that were used to make it. Each label should allow Burnfield to decipher all this information. However, she says that 'they're done at the last minute and I tend to forget what they mean.' The final meaning of *Darwin's Box* is left to whoever is looking at it. Burnfield says: 'I'm not entirely sure what these things are myself. I'm very happy for people to interpret them however they like.'

BECKY EARLEY

Becky Earley was born in Marlborough, Wiltshire, UK, in 1970. She studied Fashion and Textiles at Loughborough College of Art and Design, then moved to London to complete an MA in Fashion at Central St Martin's College of Art and Design. In 1999 she won the Peugeot Design Award in the Textiles category. Earley's work has been shown in exhibitions around Europe and in the USA, and her fashion designs have been worn to awards ceremonies by the singer Björk and the celebrity, Zoe Ball, among others. She currently teaches Textiles and Design for the Environment at the Chelsea College of Art, London.

Imaginative techniques

Earley's work in fashion and textiles is distinguished by the use of imaginative techniques linked to practical applications. One of her best-known techniques is the use of **photogram** printing, which transfers life-size images on to fabric. Earley developed the technique while studying for her MA at Central St Martin's. All the machines in the school's studio were busy, apart from the **heat transfer** machine. Earley says 'it was so old and huge and dusty that I don't think anyone wanted to risk using it'. She remembered hearing as a child about Fox Talbot, a Victorian inventor who developed the first cameras and photographic film, and who came from the same part of Wiltshire as she did. Fox Talbot also came up with a technique called 'sinotype printing', which allowed the transfer of images on to cloth. Earley developed a modern version called photogram printing, allowing her to transfer the life-sized shapes of flowers, photographs, textures – almost anything – on to fabric.

The ghostly images of photogram printing look rather like X-rays. Among its uses are 100 gowns Earley designed for use by cancer patients at the Queen Elizabeth Centre for the Treatment of Cancer in Birmingham. The gowns used images of **homeopathic** plants with perceived healing properties as their printed designs.

Photogram printing

Photogram printing is done by first treating the fabric being used with chemicals, in a place away from the light. The fabric is then overlaid with an object or objects – flowers, leaves or another fabric, for example. Finally the fabric is exposed to the light, leaving behind a ghostly impression of the original object.

Environmental textiles

Photogram printing is one of the least environmentally damaging types of printing. The fabric used for Earley's hospital gowns was also environmentally friendly, as it was made from recycled plastic bottles.

Another, more recent piece of work shows Earley's interest in textiles work that is linked to its environment. Earley became involved in a project to design wallpaper for Poltimore House, an old Tudor house in Devon that was to be renovated. The walls of the house were covered in layer after layer of wallpaper. Each layer represented years of history, with wars being fought, governments changing, and fashions coming and going between the layers.

Current work

Earley's current work continues her interest in the environmental impact of textiles and fashion design. She reuses old clothes and offcuts from the industrial process to customize ordinary garments and make them individual. She is also working on clothes designs that need less cleaning, since washing machines have an impact on the environment through using water and detergents. Among these designs are tops, where the sleeves join the body lower down the arm, away from the armpit, so that they don't get sweaty and therefore need washing less frequently.

Earley also works on large public art **commissions**; among the latest is a garden design and collection for the Eden Project in Cornwall. She also focuses on natural dyes that can be taken from plants in the project, indigo for example.

The key challenge for fashion textile designers is fashion's focus on high-speed consumption: new products every season, which people are encouraged to buy as a replacement for their 'old' clothes. This cycle of new clothes is extremely powerful and hard to break [because we] use fashion to meet basic emotional needs such as establishing our personal identity, showing membership of a group and expressing our creativity. BECKY EARLEY

Poltimore project

In 2002, Earley and two friends decided to spend a day at Poltimore House, in Devon working to create textiles and designs that were a response to the environment in which they were made.

Earley's blackberry-print suit.

One of the simplest and most striking pieces Earley created was a suit featuring splashes of bright purple and red colours. This was made by pressing plain fabric into blackberries that had been picked from a nearby hedge.

No two blackberry stains came out the same, giving the fabric a unique design. Now there are plans to **digitize** the pattern and turn it into a polka-dot print.

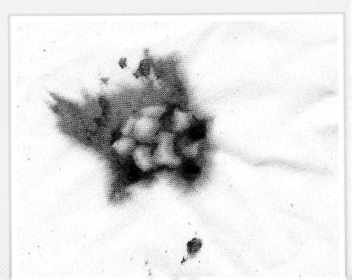

This spray-painted suit uses a pattern of ivy leaves.

A second design used ivy leaves that had been growing inside the house to make a patterned suit. The leaves were held against the fabric and sprayed with car paint, creating an outline of ivy growing up and around the legs and arms of the person wearing the suit.

The third design to come out of the day at Poltimore was inspired by the house's imposing double staircase. Imagining the grand entrances made by the heroines of Jane Austen novels in just such a setting, Earley set to work on making a ball gown for one of her friends. The gown was made from that day's newspaper, which had already been used to stop spray paint from covering the floor and so had a pattern on it. Pieces of paper were stuck together, then folded and cut to fit. In the end Earley had made a newspaper *toile*. A *toile* is a dress made entirely of **calico**, used by **couture** designers (dressmakers at the cutting edge of fashion) to make sure that they have the design exactly right, before they use expensive fabrics in the final garment.

JO GORDON

Jo Gordon was born in Glasgow, Scotland, in 1967. She was brought up away from the city, near Loch Lomond, and from an early age was interested in art. Her mother, a painter, encouraged Gordon's interest, but it was textiles rather than painting that sparked Jo's greatest enthusiasm, and her A-level piece was a sewn **appliqué** collar. Gordon is a former winner of the New Generation Award, and has exhibited at London Fashion Week – where her scarves were hung on an old door frame, for want of a proper stand, but still gathered orders worth about £20,000.

Early work

Gordon studied Sculpture at Aberdeen University, with Printing as a second subject. When she finished her degree she began a job at Ankara University, Turkey, having fallen in love with the country while on a holiday there. As well as teaching, Gordon continued to work on her own sculpture and exhibited in private galleries. She was also interested in fashion textiles, and would take her sketches to a tailor for him to make up her designs. One day he asked 'Who draws these rubbish pictures for you?' and she was too embarrassed to admit the truth – that the drawings were her own!

The combination of sculpture and fashion led Gordon to return to England to complete a Royal College of Art course in Millinery (hat making). Her training as a sculptor meant that she approached millinery from a different point of view. Gordon has made sculpture-influenced hats for **couture** shows by some of the world's most famous designers: Thierry Mugler, Comme des Garcons, Yohji Yamamoto and Hussein Chalayan.

> [Gordon's] sculptural couture hats include wonderfully tiny top hats, dolphin tails and spirals... much of her work has a sculptural quality, which goes back to her initial training [as a sculptor].
> MARIE O'MAHONEY AND SARAH E BRADDOCK, *FABRIC OF FASHION*, 2000.

Inspiration from the past

Gordon's first big independent commercial success was a knitted copy of her father's favourite, oldest hat. Echoes of the past are still a feature of Gordon's work. Her scarves and hats draw inspiration from past fashions of the 20th century – any time from the 1920s to the 1970s, but in particular the 1950s.

Jo Gordon's hats and scarves are part of a textiles range that has earned her work on Hollywood movies, as well as awards and prizes.

Traditional Scottish patterns are a key influence in Jo Gordon's work. 'I love the idea of the yarns being made and dyed individually, so that the colours in them were probably never repeated again', she says.

Felt Hairstyles

Gordon's series of pieces called *Felt Hairstyles* (2000) combines several of the key influences that are apparent in her work. The 'hairstyles' are actually a combination of hairstyle and hat, made from peach-bloom felt. They look sculptural, with clean lines and a simple shape. Many of the shapes also carry echoes of the short, neat haircuts of the 1920s, when girls began to have their hair cut short for the first time, much to the horror of their parents.

Making a Jo Gordon felt hairstyle

1 The basic material is a felt hat, which Gordon gets mail order from a company in Luton, UK. Similar hats are available mail order over the Internet. Gordon uses two basic styles of hat: caplain and hood. Hood hats fit quite close to the head and are better for the 'shorter', neater hairstyles. Caplain hats are more flared out and better for 'bigger' hairstyles. Gordon uses hats made of peach-bloom felt, which is the best quality material.

2 Gordon sprays water inside the hat to wet it, then holds the hat over a kettle of boiling water to heat the material. Felt is made using heated wool, so this reverses the process and makes the felt more flexible. It becomes possible to stretch the shape of the hat into a different form.

3 Next Gordon uses a specialist head-shaped dummy to stretch the hat down and make it more fitted to the sides and back of the head.

4 She then chalks out the shape that is to be cut into the hat. Once a 'fringe' has been cut in and it's possible to see out, Gordon puts the hat on her own head, so she can see clearly how the chalked-in shape will actually work.

5 Then Gordon cuts out the shape. 'Snipping is no good, because you end up with a ragged edge that looks like a bad haircut' says Gordon. 'You have to use long, confident strokes with the scissors.'

6 To tidy up the hat/hairstyle, Gordon sands the cut edges with fine sandpaper so that they look as smooth as possible.

7 Finally, some of the hairstyles have stitching added. Gordon originally used obvious, blanket-style stitches in simple patterns for the first versions. She now says that they could just as well have featured other additions that would individualize the shapes.

Current work

Jo Gordon now produces her own fashion range of scarves, gloves, ponchos and sweaters. In 2002 her summer collection was designed partly on computer, using scanned-in images of summer insects such as butterflies. All the wool for these pieces comes from Scotland.

As part of her fashion work, Gordon designed all the knitwear for Penélope Cruz in *Captain Corelli's Mandolin* and for the film *Neverland*, about the life of *Peter Pan* author J.M. Barrie. Meanwhile she continues to win awards: in 1997 her millinery designs were shortlisted for the Jerwood Prize (textiles) and in 1999 she won the Three Bags Full Knitwear Award at the Chelsea Crafts Fair in London.

RACHAEL HOWARD

Rachael Howard – who describes herself as an 'artist, designer and craftsperson rolled into one' – was born in 1969 in Higher Bebington, Cheshire, UK. She studied Art and Design, first at Wirral Metropolitan, then at Loughborough College of Art and Design. Howard was one of a group of six students who were the first ever **Embroidery** postgraduates at the Royal College of Art (1990–92). Her art has been exhibited in many cities, and she has received awards from the British Crafts Council and others. In 1997 she was shortlisted for the Jerwood Prize for Applied Arts.

Tie-tastic!

Howard is probably best known for her ties, which mix sketching, printing and stitching in a unique way. The ties have appeared – by virtue of having been worn by celebrities and presenters – on TV news programmes and awards shows. They are also the subject of a video featuring the proud owners of some of the ties – including the poet John Hegley – speaking about them. Howard ties have even been featured in the British soap opera, 'Brookside', where they were described as 'bloody awful' by one of the characters (who was clearly not an art lover!).

When Howard's work was spotted by the fashion designer Paul Smith he asked her to make some ties for his shop in London: Howard now says she thinks people 'bought the ties because it was a cheap way of getting a piece of my art'!

Swimmers

Howard's work often shows subjects drawn from everyday life. Since childhood she has always loved to sketch, especially people – how they stand and move, the expressions on their faces and the clothes they wear. This interest in sketching led Howard to develop a unique way of working, which keeps the energetic lines and rough shapes of a sketch in her final pieces of work. The collection of ties called *Swimmers* (1998) shows Howard's fascination with ordinary people very clearly, combined with her special technique (see page 26).

Swimmers began when Howard was asked by the British Crafts Council to complete some work with a seaside theme. Inspiration came from a series of day trips to old-fashioned British seaside resorts like Clacton in Essex. Drawing people at the English seaside produced a series of sketches, which combined various body shapes with a range of swimsuit fabrics. Howard rejects the idea that an artist's sketches are only a starting point, to be used as the basis for a piece of printing, **weaving**, painting or some other 'finished' product. Instead she uses **silk-screen printing** to transfer the sketch direct to a piece of fabric, 'colouring in with pieces of fabric', as she puts it. Finally, outlines and definition are added to the piece using visible stitching.

Making a Rachael Howard tie

1 First Howard makes pencil sketches, like the one on the right, of the subject to be featured. These work best if they are made up of simple lines that convey the shape and, if relevant, movement of the subject.

2 Then she makes a mask of the sketch so that it can be printed using silk-screen printing. Using this printing technique means it is possible to make several copies of the sketch that are almost exactly the same.

3 Next Howard chooses the fabrics that will appear in the final piece, picking colours for hair, skin, clothes, shoes and so on.

4 She prints the sketch on the base fabric (the tie) and on the fabrics chosen to make up the final piece.

5 Howard then cuts out the relevant parts of the sketch shape – the swimming-trunk shape from the swimming-trunk fabric, or the hair shape from the hair fabric, for example.

6 Then she pieces together the jigsaw of fabrics to make the whole image. These are stuck down on the base fabric using a special material that sticks fabrics together once they have been ironed with a hot iron.

7 Howard then stitches the fabrics down so that they do not lift, and prints the original sketch over the top of the fabric image.

8 Finally she uses stitching to recreate the lines of the original sketch and add detail and shading.

For *Swimmers*, the additional bits and pieces of text that appear on the base fabric of the ties were taken from seaside postcards, which were then silk-screen printed on the fabric. Adding these extra points of interest, additional subjects that catch the eye, is typical of Howard's multi-layered technique.

Indian Embroidery Factory

Howard's use of this multi-layered technique is not limited to pieces of clothing. She also uses it to produce, among other things, large wall hangings. The best known of these were the product of a trip she made to India. *Indian Embroidery Factory* (1995), for example, records a visit to a factory in New Delhi. The piece records the stages involved in making an embroidered cotton nightdress, and has recently been bought by the Museum of Science and Industry in Berlin.

Influences and inspirations

Howard has been influenced and inspired by a wide range of artists, but among those whose work she most admires are '**outsider artists**' – people who have developed their own styles and techniques outside those of official art courses. Other inspirations include the 'early, more sketchy' David Hockney (b. 1937), and the sketches of the Swiss artist Giacometti (1901–66). The figures in *Swimmers*, with their extra-long limbs and exaggerated shapes, resemble some of Giacometti's sculptures.

Current work

Howard is currently involved in a variety of projects, including work with the fashion designer Paul Smith, **commissioned** art projects for public spaces, and working with schools.

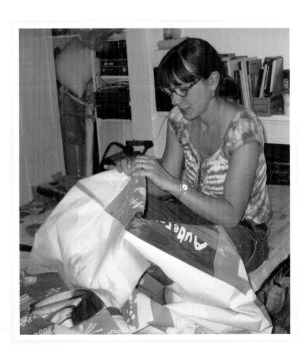

Rachael Howard shown stitching one of her recent projects.

HIKARU NOGUCHI

Hikaru Noguchi was born in Tokyo, Japan in 1967. Her father was an **interior designer** who travelled widely in the course of his work, and he used to buy knitwear from around the world on his journeys.

Today Noguchi's own award-winning knitwear is still influenced by the traditional designs her father brought back from Scandinavia and Europe.

Noguchi has worked for various companies and fashion designers, including Matthew Williamson, Kookai, Paul Smith Women and Nicole Farhi. Her work is known for its close attention to the texture and pattern of the knitted fabrics she uses. A trademark feature of Noguchi's work is the use of a variety of techniques to add relief (shape), as well as colour, to knitted fabrics. One good example of this is the shaggy scarves for which she first became well known.

Inspirations

Noguchi often works from old **knitting** pattern books she has discovered, which date from the 1930s onwards. She is particularly interested in traditional patterns and techniques that are disappearing from use, for example some traditional Scandinavian patterns and knitting methods.

Noguchi's textiles often combine techniques and designs from a variety of places: a Peruvian knit with a Scandinavian design but using Fair-Isle colours, for example, or a Welsh blanket using Andean shapes.

Noguchi's work uses a variety of methods to give her fabrics texture and shape. Plain-knitted base fabrics are sometimes accompanied by lacy knitting and crochet techniques in unique combinations.

> *Being a **graphic designer** sounded like a cool job. But I found the colours and textures I could use were dull and flat. Studying textiles offered me the chance to work in so many different ways, which is why I changed to studying Constructed Textiles.*
> HIKARU NOGUCHI

Shaggy bags

Noguchi's shaggy bags are made using a unique process, combining a plain knitted base fabric with a special kind of wool called '**slub yarn**'. Slub yarn has varying thickness, ranging from the size of ordinary wool to the thickness of a man's thumb. This variation in thickness is crucial to the technique of making the bags.

First Noguchi begins the base fabric: this is knitted on a machine. At the tenth row, a double section of the slub yarn is cut (two 'bulges' of thicker fabric linked together by a thinner section). Then Noguchi sews the ends into the base fabric and cuts the loop linking them, so that each bulge of slub hangs down alone. Ten rows later, more bulges of slub are sewn into the base fabric in the same way. In the end, the fabric comes out looking shaggy-coated and tactile. The amount of slub Noguchi sews into the base fabric determines whether the shaggy cloth is thick and bulging or thin and straggly.

JESSICA OGDEN

Jessica Ogden is known for making simple, functional garments that re-use **vintage** fabrics. She was born in Jamaica in 1970, and her interest in clothes goes back to the different garments that she remembers people wearing during her childhood. Her work has been exhibited in London, Prague, Antwerp and Tokyo, and her one-off pieces have been worn by the singer Tori Amos, among others.

Ogden is best known today for clothes that are handmade and individual, rather than being **mass-produced**. Her approach to fashion and textiles is almost opposite that of much of the high fashion industry, which needs people to buy new clothes before their old ones are worn out.

Ogden is also well known for her **installations**, including 1999's *Glimpse*. In this a warehouse attic was used to display an interactive exhibition. Visitors could open doors and drawers to discover pieces of Ogden's work hidden inside. Her live shows during London Fashion Week have also caught the attention of the world's media.

> *I see the clothes as having a much longer life than a six-month trend. I see the fabric I use as having already had a life... You can read the history: the little pieces of **embroidery**, the mending, and the caring they've received.* JESSICA OGDEN

Favourite patchwork dress

Ogden's work is inspired by the fabrics she hunts down for use in her garments. The fabrics that provide a starting point are sometimes old, worn thin or torn. Ogden stitches them, **quilts** them, adds layers and patches to create a new, unique textile from the old. One benefit of this for Ogden is that she can mix fabrics from various times and places, each of which has its own history.

A good example of this is Ogden's favourite patchwork dress. The dress shows many of the themes that recur in Ogden's work: an old garment used in combination with pieces of vintage or unusual cloth, all reworked using hand stitching to her own pattern. The basic garment is an old patchwork dress from the 1950s. Where areas of the original dress had become worn with age, they have been covered over with new patches, sometimes using fabrics that are much older than the basic garment.

Ogden is always looking for interesting fabrics to use in her work. Friends search mainly in the second-hand clothes markets of London, but people in Tokyo, Paris and a variety of other cities keep their eyes peeled for things that Ogden might use. These are then kept in her studio until she finds the right use for them. Sometimes they might wait a long time before being used; the favourite patchwork dress waited so long that Ogden can't now remember where it originally came from.

Influences

One of the biggest influences on Ogden's work is her mum: 'I remember her sewing clothes for herself and for us when I was a child, and some of those clothes still inspire me.' Ogden is also influenced by Eastern styles of clothing: she loves the simple, functional approach to clothing used in China and Japan. 'It's a very simple approach: wrapping something around your body or folding it.'

FRAN REED

Fran Reed is an American textile artist. She was born in La Jolla, California in 1943, and studied Art Education at the University of Oregon. She is most famous for her basketry work, which has been widely exhibited in the USA and Europe. Reed's art has won a variety of awards, including the Lila Wallace Reader's Digest Fellowship, which led to a three-month residency in Monet's gardens in Giverny, France. She teaches basketry workshops and has lectured in Alaskan Native Arts at the Alaska Pacific University. Since 1969 Reed has lived and worked in Anchorage, Alaska.

Fish skin baskets

Reed is best known for making baskets using fish skins and gut. The native people of Alaska and other sub-Arctic regions traditionally put these materials to a variety of uses. Reed herself says that she's 'greatly inspired by traditional Native craftwork.' Although she does not use traditional techniques, Reed has adapted Native materials for use in her striking baskets. Sometimes the names of the baskets echo the animals from which they are made: *Entertwined for the Halibut* (made from halibut skin), *Rock the Innernet* (rockfish) or *Sockeye on the Web* (red salmon, sometimes called sockeye salmon), for example. Other baskets, like *Behemoth*, reflect the history and culture of the Alaskan region.

A collection of Reed's unique fish skin baskets.

Behemoth

The *Behemoth* basket (2002) is one of a series of four pieces of art that Reed produced because of her interest in whales. The word 'behemoth' means an enormous creature: Reed says that 'like the whale this is a large yet simple form and I find it to be very strong.' In the northern part of Alaska, where people traditionally live mainly by hunting, the whale is one of the most important sources of food for the Inupiat people. When the hunters have killed a whale, all the villagers come to the shore to help pull the whale from the sea. The meat is cut from its body in long vertical strips that run down the side of the whale. The shape, colours and textures of *Behemoth* reflect this traditional method of stripping the meat from a whale. The interior of the basket is made of animal gut, which when wet can be moulded to a particular shape. Inside the gut are ribs and other **armatures** (things to make a framework for the basket). These are made of willow or black bamboo.

The outer skin of the basket is made from halibut skin, which Reed chose because its skin has black and white areas. Mostly black skin was used, except for one strip on the side of the basket. Here, white skin echoes the area where the Inupiat might have started stripping the flesh from a whale's body.

Technique

Reed modestly says that her technique is 'pretty simple. First I catch a fish! Usually that's actually my husband's job…' In fact, Reed's technique is probably unique, since she developed it herself through trial and error.

Once it has been caught and brought to the studio, the fish is skinned. A cut is made either along the belly or down the side, and then the skin is taken off by stripping it away with a sharp blade. The fin bones and tailbone are cut inside the skin with shears, so that they stay in position on the fish skin. Then Reed uses a scalpel to strip all the flesh out of the fin and tail sections. To do the same job on the rest of the skin she uses an *ulu* knife, a curved knife used by the native peoples of Alaska.

When all the flesh has been stripped away, the skin is sprinkled with chemicals that help draw out the oils that fish skins normally contain. The skin is then put in a freezer. Once enough skins have been gathered they can be stitched together in the right shape to make the outer layer of a basket.

Gut maché

Before the skins are stitched together, Reed uses a form – something like a balloon, for example – to help her make the basket's shape from animal gut. The gut comes in sheets from a sausage supply merchant. It has to be washed and cleaned carefully before use, to make sure there is no salt left in it. Then the water-soaked gut is cut into strips, which can be layered on to the form. One of the secrets to this part of the technique is patience. Reed says: 'I always consider time and gravity. The gut needs to be dry before I can turn the form over, and it will slide off if I put too much on before letting it dry. It works just like *papier maché*, and I often call it 'gut *maché*'.'

At this stage designs can be added by drawing, painting or layering in things like seaweed, leaves or pressed flowers. Both the gut and the fish skin that will be added next allow light through, so these additions will be visible in the finished basket. Armatures of cane, willow or driftwood are also added, so that the basket does not collapse when the inner form is removed.

Stitching the skin

After the gut shape has been finished, the fish skins can be stitched into place. Reed adds this layer using waxed linen thread and curved leather needles. Although the gut shrinks as it dries, the fish skin shrinks more, so the two layers become tightly bound together. Once the inside of the basket has been sealed with a clear acrylic, it is finished.

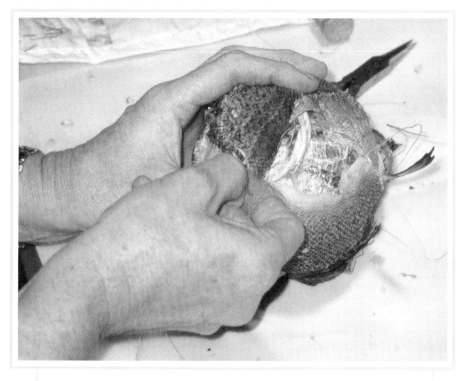

Reed at work stitching one of her basket sculptures. Reed is an Alaskan artist who makes baskets out of materials native to her environment. In 1989 she was inducted into the Tsimshian Killer Whale Clan.

All the fish have their attributes. The rockfish are spiny and tough, the king salmon are thick and hard to stitch, the halibut shrink in their own special way. I made one piece out of wolf eel and found it to be an absolutely beautiful 'fabric'. I'd love to do more, but have a hard time coming by them … I guess I don't have a favourite; it all depends on what I'm trying to do. FRAN REED

SOPHIE ROET

Sophie Roet was born in Melbourne, Australia in 1969. When she was eleven years old her parents moved to London. 'Our whole family went over for what was meant to be a year of travelling,' she says, 'but we never returned.' Roet is now well known as the creator of innovative new fabrics, including light, seemingly fragile cloths made of gossamer-like threads, as well as an amazing textile that bonds fashion fabrics to metallic sheeting. Her awards include the Lea and Bullukian Textile Competition in France.

Roet obtained an M.A. in Woven Textile Design at the Royal College of Art in London from 1993 to 1995. After this she went to work in Paris before returning to London in 1998 to set up her own studio. Today the studio is a laboratory for the creation of new textiles. These include experimental material for exhibitions and woven textiles for fashion designers around the world. Fabrics created by Roet have stalked down the catwalks during the fashion shows of designers such as John Galliano, Gianni Versace and Alexander McQueen.

A detail of Roet's Water *(1999), the fabric that first made her famous for creating innovative new materials.*

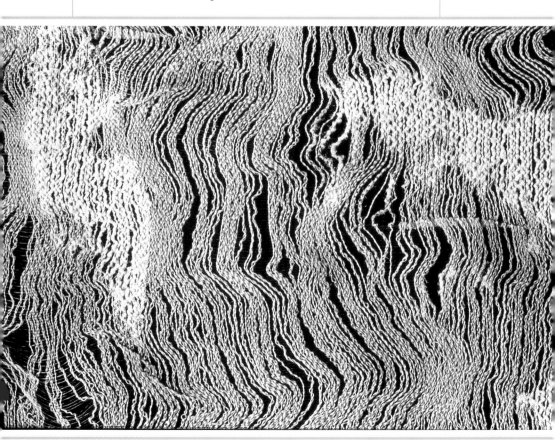

Water

One of Roet's first big successes was a fabric she designed for Hussein Chalayan while still at the Royal College of Art, called *Water*. Her work often draws inspiration from Japanese textiles – she loves their simplicity and the willingness of Japanese weavers to use modern yarns with traditional techniques.

Water drew its inspiration from *mizugoromo*, or 'water cloth'. This textile moves in a way that reminds people of the movement of waves on the surface of the water. *Mizugoromo* is a traditional Japanese cloth made by manipulating the **weft yarn** (the yarn that is woven across the loom) using special irregular reeds. Some Japanese weavers even cut a notch into the nail of their middle finger and use this to comb the fabric instead of using reeds. This manipulation of the cloth creates an irregular, wavy movement of the weft threads. The final fabric was worn at important ceremonies, as a transparent layer over another **kimono**.

Roet's version of *mizugoromo* fabric developed this process even further. She manipulated the yarn to create a final fabric that was blue and green, and woven with a mixture of artificial **fibre** and cotton. Roet then used a devoré technique to remove the cotton. This is a process where a chemical mixture is printed or painted on to the cloth and then pressed using great heat. The cotton fibres are burned away, leaving just the artificial ones behind. *Water* was used by Hussein Chalayan as an overdress; the fabric beneath it glowed in the dark, shining through the gaps in the material.

Recent work

The inspiration for Roet's recent work came from microscopic pictures of the structures of plants and animals. She uses the technical qualities of the threads she uses to mirror an effect found in the natural world. The finished fabric carries echoes of a creature known as *Aequorea victoria* – a tiny jellyfish that is farmed by **biotechnologists** to obtain the fluorescent proteins it produces. Like the fabric, the jellyfish's fluorescence allows it to glow in the dark.

Roet's *Wandering Lines* pieces are apparently woven of white, yellow and pale blue threads, in a textile that looks not unlike her earlier *Water*. But *Wandering Lines* has a secret life, which is only revealed in the dark. Once the lights are turned out, the fabric shows its alternative colours – brilliant greens and blues that range from a vibrant electric colour to a restful royal blue. The effect is achieved by **weaving** the fabric using see-through threads that can easily be made to take a particular shape, along with polyester threads that have been treated to glow colourfully in the dark. The meandering threads of *Wandering Lines* also provide a reminder of the tentacles that some jellyfish trail behind them as they drift through the sea.

Metal Dresses

Roet's work often features combinations of natural and artificial fibres, producing an apparently simple material that is actually the result of a lot of hard work and experimentation. One good example of this is her recent fabric called *Metal Dresses* (2000).

To create *Metal Dresses*, Roet worked with a company called CS Interglas. Normally this company produces hi-tech materials for use in buildings, aircraft manufacture and other industrial processes. The leap to working with a fashion textile designer must have been quite a stretch. One of CS Interglas's specialities is a process that bonds glass fibre textiles to metal sheeting, and it was this that Roet wanted to adapt for use in fashion textiles.

Technique

The starting point for the fabric was a length of thin metallic sheeting. This was rolled on to the laboratory table and covered on one side with special glue. The glue was allowed to dry for about five minutes, then silk fabric was rolled across the top of it. This was ironed with an ordinary household iron. The heat of the iron helped the glue to fix itself to the fabric and the metal sheet. Finally the newly made textile was turned over so that the whole process could be repeated on the other side. Without this last stage anyone wearing a piece of clothing made using the fabric would feel as though they were wearing metal clothes!

The end result of this process is a fabric that feels comfortable enough to wear, but can be shaped into almost any design. A dress that has been crumpled will retain its crumpled look; creases and pleats stay in place until they are folded out smooth again.

> *I was interested in creating a hand-woven textile length. I wanted to make very delicate, simple, feminine fashion textiles and then charge them with a new hidden quality through a metallic bonding process. Just imagine folding a soft pale pink satin textile and finding that it holds it shape without help. Tightly crumple a silk* **organza** *dress and find it remains in its tightly crumpled state!*
> SOPHIE ROET

NORMAN SHERFIELD

Norman Sherfield is an American textile artist based in Los Angeles, California. He was born in Leavenworth, Kansas in 1948. At school Sherfield was 'always interested in science. I had microscopes and chemistry kits for Christmas presents.' On leaving school in 1966 he joined the US Navy, spending three years on a helicopter carrier off the coast of Vietnam. After this the navy paid for him to go to college, first in Los Angeles to study Zoology, then to Sonoma State College to study Social Sciences.

During the 1970s Sherfield became involved in the art scene. He spent eight years in San Francisco and New York. In 1983 he returned to California, settling in Los Angeles and discovered 'the technique which has consumed me – knotting.'

Knotting

Sherfield is best known for his sculptural shapes made using a basketry technique called knotting. This uses a simple overhand knot, which is made around a core of waxed linen threads. Sherfield's artwork uses variations on this simple, labour-intensive technique to produce different shapes and textures, as well as using a variety of colours. The pieces are knotted around an object – in the smaller ones these are often small stones, which are left inside the finished piece. The larger pieces are knotted around things like larger stones, bottles, plastic toys and bits of plastic, which are usually taken out once the piece is finished. The end effect of this is that the smaller pieces often weigh more than their larger cousins. Even a small piece can contain thousands of knots.

Waxed Linen Boll Weaver, Larval Stage *(2001) is an example of Sherfield's knotting. There is another* Boll Weaver, *made in the same year, at the 'adult' stage.*

*The simplicity of the basic knot, combined with the repetitive nature of knotting, is meditative and allows me to immerse myself in the work. As each knot is tied, it is as though a pulse is added to the form, as though I am breathing life into the weave. The sculptures grow as I work on them, forming baskets or containers of potential life in **symbolic** form.* NORMAN SHERFIELD

Metamorphosis

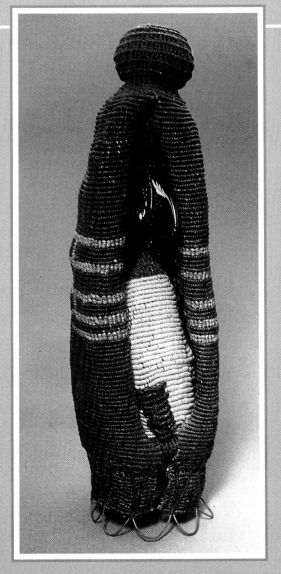

Metamorphosis (2001) consists of a knotted shape with a smaller rock at the top, then an open cavity slit down the middle of the knotted shape. Into this has been placed a rock with a beak-like part of a plastic toy superhero attached. The entire piece is supported by wire. The stone inside can be removed but is intended to remain in place.

One of the people to influence Sherfield's ideas is the composer John Cage, who thinks that patterns can be generated using chance. There is always an element of chance in one of Sherfield's pieces, even down to sometimes choosing colour combinations based on the roll of a dice.

A similar element of chance is involved in the additions to the basic shape that feature in Sherfield's pieces. Generally he just adds something when it feels right: 'In most cases I have small objects I've found and/or stones in my pocket which are incorporated into the work as I feel something is needed.' *Metamorphosis* is an excellent example of the role of chance in Sherfield's work.

Part of a series

Metamorphosis was originally created as the third of a series of pieces of art that had all been knotted around the same large stone, which was removed from each piece as it was finished and then used for the next one. Unfortunately, Sherfield 'accidentally knotted too far' and was unable to take the stone out for reuse. He wanted to get it back in order to be able to carry on the series, and the only way to do this was to cut the original piece of work open. 'So I slit a hole up one side, removed the stone and took off some other smaller stones that were attached to the larger piece.'

Acccidental inspiration

The slit-open piece cried out to be developed into something else. So Sherfield began to work on a smaller stone that he planned to place inside the slit-open form. He added a beak-like plastic arm from a superhero toy to the stone, making it look as though an animal inside is splitting open the larger form to release itself. The piece conjures up images of a snake sloughing off its skin or a chick breaking out of an egg.

Metamorphosis is about change; the way one form can completely metamorphose into an entirely different existence. 'Is it done now?' Sherfield asked himself. 'Only time will determine that!'

Sherfield says, 'The larger creature appears more solid and stable, and the new creature appears to be ready to fly off leaving its old shell and discover a different stage of its existence.'

Influences

The main source of inspiration for Sherfield's work is the natural world. His basic forms, like those of Penny Burnfield (see pages 12–15), are **organic** shapes inspired by biology or fossilized shapes from prehistory. These are then developed along the lines of images from dreams and imagination – the final meaning of the pieces is left to the person looking at it to decide.

Sherfield also draws inspiration from different art forms and styles from around the world. Native American, tribal African and Aboriginal influences can be seen in some of his pieces.

In terms of actual artists, Sherfield says his 'first influence would be Dominic Di Mare, a papermaker and sculptor from the 1960s'. Art movements that provide inspiration include the Dadaists, a group of artists based in Switzerland during and after World War I. They chose their name (which is the French word for a child's rocking horse) at random from a dictionary, and were deliberately against the art world in general and art that made 'sense' in particular.

Future directions

Some of Sherfield's most recent work has involved making objects that have taken a more human form. This includes the pieces *Des Ana*, *Sentinel* and *Bricoleur*. He has also begun to make his art more multi-layered, so that an inner layer to some pieces exists. He says that 'part of the work disappears and is only known to be there by me, the maker.'

YINKA SHONIBARE

Yinka Shonibare was born in London in 1962. His parents were originally from Nigeria, and at the age of four they returned with him to live there. Shonibare's first memories of art classes were at primary school in Nigeria. At seventeen Shonibare returned to England to finish his A-level examinations. Following that he began an Art Foundation course at the Wimbledon College of Art, but after three weeks was forced to leave. Shonibare had been struck by the rare disease, transverse myelitis, which left him paralysed from the neck down.

The next three years were spent in partial recovery from the disease, though Shonibare still suffers some effects from it today. But he was able to join a course in Painting at the Byamshaw School of Art in London. A tutor suggested that he should explore 'his own' background in his work, by which he meant Shonibare's African background. As a black Englishman who had spent part of his life living in Nigeria, Shonibare felt that 'his own' background was far richer and more complex than the tutor meant to imply. The art for which he first became famous – including pieces from the *Dressing Down* exhibition – reflected this richness and diversity.

Mr and Mrs Andrews Without Their Heads

The seeds of Shonibare's 1999 exhibition, *Dressing Down*, were sown by a visit to Brixton market in South London. Brixton is home to people from many different cultures – from London, other parts of Europe, Africa and the Caribbean among other places. The market has stalls selling fabrics from all parts of the world, and Shonibare went there to look at African prints, in the hope that they would be useful in his paintings. Speaking to the stallholders, he discovered that the 'African' fabrics he was holding were actually made in The Netherlands or in Hyde, Manchester. Fabrics that combined Africanness and Englishness seemed to resonate with his own background in some way, and Shonibare began to use the patterns in his paintings.

Double Dutch

Shonibare's visit to Brixton market first gave rise to a set of paintings on African fabrics called *Double Dutch* (1994). Some of the ideas in *Double Dutch* were developed further for the *Dressing Down* exhibition. In these works, vibrantly coloured pieces of African fabric have been sewn into the shape of clothes worn by the English ruling classes at the time they began their **colonization** of Africa. One of the most striking pieces is based on the painting *Mr and Mrs Andrews* (1748–49) by Thomas Gainsborough. Gainsborough's painting shows a man standing next to a seated woman, with the English landscape rolling away from them into the distance. Shonibare's version, *Mr and Mrs Andrews Without Their Heads* (1998), shows two headless figures, dummies made of bronze and fibreglass, which have been arranged in the same poses. They are similarly dressed, but their clothes are made of brilliant-coloured African prints, rather than the plain colours in the original.

Mr and Mrs Andrews *(1748–49) by Thomas Gainsborough.*

Like much of Shonibare's work, *Mr and Mrs Andrews Without Their Heads* reflects the links between the English ruling classes and their colonial subjects. Much of the rulers' wealth ultimately came from the colonies, through the slave trade, Caribbean sugar plantations, Indian cotton and **jute** manufacture, and other colonial businesses. The headlessness of the figures 'deracializes them', as Shonibare puts it. It also provides an echo of the **French Revolution** of 1789, during which many French aristocrats were beheaded by revolutionaries.

Production process

Producing the pieces that made up the *Dressing Down* exhibition was a long process from Shonibare's first visit to Brixton market. Having become interested in the fabric, he visited London's Victoria and Albert Museum to look at the books in the museum's costume department. He would sketch, or sometimes photocopy, patterns, then fill in indications of which African fabrics should be used for the piece. Working with a theatrical costumier (someone who makes clothes for the theatre), Shonibare then oversaw the production of the dresses and suits for *Dressing Down*. He supervised every stage of the work to make sure it was true to his original conception.

> *African fabric signifies African identity, rather like American jeans, Levi's, are an indicator of trendy youth culture. In Brixton, African fabric is worn with pride among radical or cool youth ... It becomes a way of holding on to one's identity in a culture presumed foreign or different. [In this sense] African fabric is a colonial construction [because it is a reaction to colonial relationships].*
> YINKA SHONIBARE.

Photographic pieces

Building on the theme Africanness in an English context, Shonibare has created a number of photographic pieces, including the five photos entitled *Diary Of A Victorian Dandy* (1998) and the twelve photos *Dorian Gray* (2001). In *Victorian Dandy*, one photo from which was used as a poster on the London Underground, Shonibare himself takes the place of the African fabrics used elsewhere. The photos show scenes taken from the life of a dandy – a man who is unduly devoted to clothes and fashion. A dandy in Victorian society was viewed poorly by 'polite' society. In the photos, Shonibare appears not only as the dandy, but also as a black man in a white context. Like a dandy in Victorian times, he appears at odds with a world that he can never quite enter.

One of the photos from Shonibare's Diary of a Victorian Dandy *(1998). The photo echoes the posed style of paintings that were popular during the Victorian age.*

Dorian Gray reproduces scenes from the 1945 film *Portrait of Dorian Gray* – the only difference is that in the photographs Shonibare has taken the place of the actor playing Dorian Gray. The novel, on which the film was based, was written by Oscar Wilde. It explores the meaning of identity and ideal beauty for the book's hero. In the photos, Shonibare's appearance again raises questions about identity.

documenta

Yinka Shonibare's work has increasingly been the subject of international attention and praise. In 2002 he was invited to exhibit a piece at the *documenta* exhibition in Kassel, Germany. *Gallantry and Criminal Conversation*, the piece shown at 'documenta', was extremely well reviewed, confirming Shonibare's place as one of the most well respected artists of today.

GEORGINA VON ETZDORF

Georgina von Etzdorf was born in Peru in 1955, but Georgina von Etzdorf is not just a person; it is also the name of a company that was started in 1981 by three friends. Today this company is known for producing textiles that draw its inspiration from the cutting edge of creative work. The people involved work closely with ideas that began life in the art world and find ways to make them work as commercial textiles.

Rubber and Slate

One example of the way in which Georgina von Etzdorf uses ideas from the world of textile art is the textile piece called *Rubber and Slate*, by B. Morrall. The piece was inspired by objects Morrall found on beaches in Pembrokeshire, Wales. These included bits of old bathmat, wood, deflated footballs, twine and slate. Trying to combine natural and artificial fibres, she developed *Rubber and Slate*. This piece used a sheet of rubber as the basic material, with different-sized pebbles of slate pushed through the rubber. When the textile is stroked it makes a gentle rattling sound, like waves lapping on the shore of a pebbly beach.

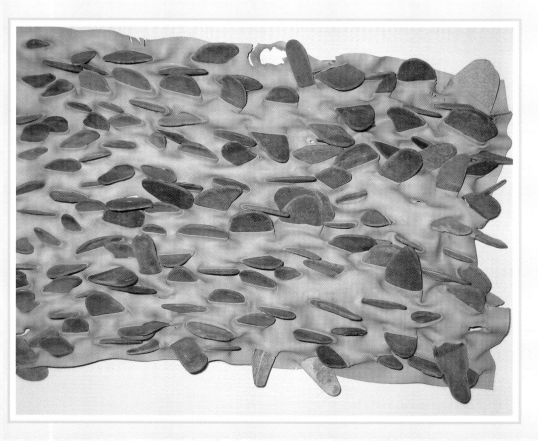

Georgina Von Etzdorf saw *Rubber and Slate* at the 'Indigo' show in Paris, and decided to buy it. The company also invited Morrall to come and develop the ideas her work contained. The textile particularly appealed to the company because it worked on more than one of the senses – not just sight, but also touch and sound, through the tinkling noise it made when stroked. This combination of different senses is one of the key themes of Georgina von Etzdorf's work.

The result of Morrall's further work was a **prototype** textile that again combined natural and artificial **fibres**. This time the piece used slate stitched with fishing line to a background fabric of iridescent **organza**.

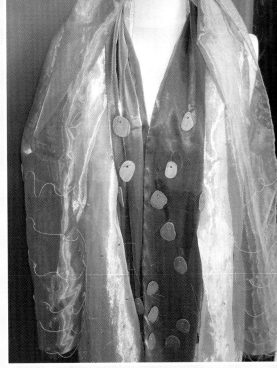

The three generations of textile that grew from the original Rubber and Slate.

This second slate fabric led to a third piece, which used a base fabric of metallic silk, which then had tiny square glass beads stitched on to it with dyed fishing line. Finally, the body of work that had begun with the textile art piece *Rubber and Slate* ended up being produced as a fashion textile. Scarves using the metallic silk fabric were made and sold as part of the Georgina von Etzdorf's Winter 1999 collection.

Future directions

The company's latest pieces include scarves that are something between being a traditional scarf and a piece of jewellery. Typical of these is *Whirlygig Necklace*, which uses wire, beads and torn strips of fabric, mostly chiffon, to create a piece that is a scarf, a piece of jewellery and a work of art all at the same time. Like *Rubber and Slate*, *Whirlygig Necklace* was another product of a spell spent at the Georgina von Etzdorf studios by a textile art student.

> *I value the things we would instantly and naturally respond to as children. They are still there and spontaneous, part of life when we grow up.*
> GEORGINA VON ETZDORF

TIMELINE

1945 World War II ends

1946 Penny Burnfield is born
Winston Churchill, British Prime Minister during World War II, warns that an 'iron curtain' is about to divide Europe. On one side will be the **communist** countries, on the other the **capitalist** ones.

1948 Norman Sherfield is born
Harry S Truman wins a shock victory in the first postwar US presidential election

1952 Michael Brennand-Wood is born
Queen Elizabeth II is crowned in London

1955 Georgina von Etzdorf is born

1962 Yinka Shonibare is born
The Beatles have their first big hit with 'Love Me Do'

1967 Jo Gordon is born
Hikaru Noguchi is born
Muhammad Ali wins the Heavyweight Boxing Championship for the second time

1968 USSR invades Czechoslovakia to remove a government that had granted the Czech people more freedom

1969 Sophie Roet is born
Rachael Howard is born
US astronauts Armstrong and Aldrin are the first humans to walk on the Moon

1970 Becky Earley is born
Jessica Ogden is born

1977 Michael Brennand-Wood '*Flags and Other Projects*' exhibition

1980 Michael Brennand-Wood '*Recent Works in Paint, Timber and Thread*' solo exhibition
The USA boycotts the Moscow Olympics, refusing to send any competitors to take part
Former Beatle John Lennon is shot dead by Mark David Chapman

1981 The Georgina von Etzdorf design partnership is formed

1982 Michael Brennand-Wood '*Fabric and Form*' group exhibition

1987 Fran Reed features in '*Innerskins/Outerskins: Gut and Fishskins*' at the San Francisco Craft and Folk Art Museum, San Francisco, California
Norman Sherfield features in *Visions from the Pacific Rim*

1990	Georgina von Etzdorf featured in *Colour into Cloth*, Cooper-Hewitt Museum, New York
	East and West Germany are reunited; Germany is no longer split in two, as it had been since the end of the World War II
1991	The Communist Party loses power in the USSR, which quickly ceases to exist
1992	Yinka Shonibare wins 'Barclays Young Artists Award'
1993	Rachael Howard solo show *Visions of India*
	Fran Reed features in *Basketry: Non-traditional Forms* at the Worth Gallery, Taos, New Mexico
1994	Becky Earley featured in *Street Style* at London's Victoria and Albert Museum
	Sophie Roet wins Woven Textile Designer Prize for *Texprint*
1995	Rachael Howard wins Daler-Rowney Award for Outstanding Sketch Books at *Art of the Stitch* Exhibition
1996	Becky Earley and Jo Gordon both win New Generation awards from British Fashion Council
	Georgina von Etzdorf awarded honorary Doctorate of Design from Winchester School of Art
1997	Jo Gordon, Michael Brennand-Wood and Rachael Howard nominated for Jerwood Prize for Applied Arts: Textiles
	Rachael Howard and Michael Brennand-Wood featured in *Art of the Stitch*, Embroiderers Guild International Open Exhibition
1998	Jo Gordon and Hikaru Noguchi featured in *Satellites of Fashion*, British Crafts Council international touring exhibition
	Sophie Roet exhibition at Museum of Textiles, Toronto
	Diary of an Edwardian Dandy (Yinka Shonibare) exhibition at the Institute of International Visual Arts, London
1999	Becky Earley wins Textile section of Peugeot Awards
	Yinka Shonibare's *Dressing Down* exhibition
1999–2001	Jessica Ogden featured in *Lost and Found*, British Council touring exhibition
2000	Yinka Shonibare's *Effective, Defective, Creative* at Science Museum, London, and *Affectionate Men* at Victoria and Albert Museum, London. Norman Sherfield features in *From Fiber to Form – The Unexpected* at Studio Channel Island Art Center, Camarillo, California.
2001	Fran Reed is Jurors Choice at the *Earth, Fire and Fiber* exhibition
2002	Yinka Shonibare features in the *documenta* exhibition at Kassel, Germany

GLOSSARY

abstract existing in thought rather than in real life. Abstract art uses shapes and colours to achieve an effect, instead of trying reproduce something recognizable from the real world.

alchemy ancient practice of trying to turn ordinary metals into gold, using complicated techniques

appliqué technique of cutting out or making pieces of fabric and then sewing them on to other fabrics to make patterns or pictures

armature framework of long, thin spikes that is used for support, almost like a rib cage

biotechnologist scientist who tries to make biological processes more profitable in industry, for example, making plants grow more quickly

calico kind of cloth

capitalist economic system in which the production and distribution of goods depend on private wealth and profit-making

colonization process of one country taking over the government of another. For example, India was colonized by the British, who took over its government and sent British people to India to occupy most of the important positions in the country.

commissioned asked to produce something to order. For example, an artist could be commissioned to produce a sculpture that will appear in a public park.

communist economic system that seeks to distribute wealth evenly in a situation of economic plenty

couture handmade, high-fashion clothes that are produced by clothes designers for special shows are called couture

digitize to make digital, or useable by a computer

embroidery art of decorating cloth using stitching

evolution process where things develop slowly over a long period of time is called evolution

felt fabric that is made from wool, which is heated and made damp, then pressed into shape

felting process of making felt

fibre kind of thread

French Revolution period of French history during the late 18th and early 19th centuries, when the French people rejected rule by their royal family and tried to set up a democratic government

graphic designer person who sets out a combination of words, pictures, photos and diagrams so that they look good

heat transfer technique for printing in which heat causes shapes to transfer from one object to another, such as a leaf on to fabric

homeopathic using homeopathy, the treating of a disease using extremely small doses of the disease itself to cure the person

installation work of art that is put together or 'installed' in a room or space – indoors or outdoors – which relies on the space as part of its effect

interior designer someone who designs the insides of buildings, including the furnishings and decoration

jute rough fibre that is sometimes made into rope, as well as sackcloth and matting

kimono traditional Japanese piece of clothing, which looks something like a very fancy dressing gown

knitting special technique of knotting together threads, often of wool or cotton, so that they make a fabric

mass-produced made in large numbers

multi-faceted made up of many parts

motif distinctive feature that is part of a pattern

notation note-taking, or the notes that result from it

organic natural growth and development or relating to nature

organza thin, stiff, semi-transparent fabric that reflects the light, used in dressmaking

'**outsider art**' art created by people who have no specialist art training

photogram picture produced using photographic materials but without using a camera

prototype first-ever version of something, made to see if it will work

pupa stage of an insect's development between larva and imago

quilt to join pieces of cloth with some sort of padding sewn between them to other, similar pieces of cloth

silk-screen printing process of printing a shape or shapes, using a screen made of silk that allows colour through in some places but not in others. This is also called serigraphy.

slub yarn woollen yarn in which each thick section is followed by a thin one

symbolic using symbols

symbols things that stand for something else. For example, some people think their country's sports teams are symbolic of the whole country – if they play well and fairly, it makes the country look good and fair.

Turner Prize annual prize given to a British artist under 50 for an outstanding exhibition or other presentation of their work

vintage in fashion, measuring a garment that dates from several years ago; from 10 to 100 years or even older

warp yarn threads that are stretched lengthwise (up and down) on a weaving loom. Other threads are woven through them to make cloth (weft yarn).

weaving process of turning thread into cloth, done using a device called a loom

weft yarn threads that are woven sideways on a weaving loom, running above and then below the threads that are stretched along it (warp yarn)

KEY WORKS

MICHAEL BRENNAND-WOOD
Howlaa (1978)
Navigator (1990)
You Are Here (1999)

PENNY BURNFIELD
I Want to be Alone (1999)
Darwin's Box (2001)

BECKY EARLEY
Commissioned evening dress for Zoe Ball at Brit Awards (1997)
Radiotherapy treatment gowns for Queen Elizabeth Hospital (1999)
Indigo Project, Eden Project Cornwall (2000–)

RACHAEL HOWARD
Indian Embroidery Factory (1995)
White Slip – Second Clothes Sort (1997)
Swimmers collection (1997–98)

HIKARU NOGUCHI SELECTED EXHIBITIONS
Solo exhibition at Senbikiya Gallery, Tokyo (1995)
Objects of Our Time, American Craft Museum New York (1998)
Contemporary Design Exhibition, Sotheby's, London (1999–2000)

FRAN REED SELECTED EXHIBITIONS
Contemporary Baskets, Thirteen Moons Gallery, Sante Fé NM (2002)
BLEU, le lin est bleu… 2nd Biennale du Lin Contemporain, Brie-Comte-Robert,
France (2001)
Baskets and Beyond, Centre for the Visual Arts, St Louis MI (1999)

SOPHIE ROET
Water Textile (1999)
Metal Textile (2000)

NORMAN SHERFIELD SELECTED EXHIBITIONS
Contemporary International Basketmaking, Whitworth Art Gallery, London
(2000)
Why Knot? Angels Gate Cultural Centre, San Pedro CA (1998)
Vessels, the Armory Center for the Arts, Pasadena CA

YINKA SHONIBARE
Double Dutch (1994)
Dressing Down (1999)
Gallantry and Criminal Conversation (2002)

WHERE TO SEE WORKS

Many artists and the galleries that exhibit their work have good web sites on which you can look at pieces of art. Often keying the artist's name into a search engine will bring up a list of sites to visit – Fran Reed at the American Art Company (www.americanartco.com) and Thirteen Moons Gallery (www.thirteenmoonsgallery.com) shows her work in this way, for example.

Textiles art tends to be shown in travelling exhibitions that start at a gallery or museum and then move to a variety of locations. The best way to find out about these is to contact your country's national arts or craft organization, which will know of exhibitions in your area.

A key venue in London is The Crafts Council at 44a Pentonville Rd, Islington, London N1 9BY, or visit the web site: www.craftscouncil.org.uk

Museums also sometimes have displays of textiles work: try the Victoria and Albert Museum in London or any Guggenheim Museum, for example.

FURTHER READING

The artists featured in each publication are shown in square brackets.

Baskets: Tradition and Beyond [Fran Reed], Kevin Wallace (Guild Books, 2000)
Contemporary International Basketmaking [Fran Reed], Merrell Holberton (British Craft Council 1999)
Dressing Down [Yinka Shonibare], (Ikon Gallery, Birmingham, 1999)
Fabric of Fashion [Becky Early, Jo Gordon, Hikaru Noguchi, Jessica Ogden, and Sophie Roet], (British Council 2000)
Georgina von Etzdorf: Sensuality, Art and Fabric, Nilgin Yusuf (Thames and Hudson, 1999)
Icebreakers: Alaska's Most Innovative Artists [Fran Reed], Julie Decker (Decker Art Service 1999)
Ideas In Weaving [Sophie Roet], Ann Sutton and Diane Sheehan (Contemporary Books, 1989)
International Textiles Magazine – October 2000 has an article on Sophie Roet
Nature In Design [Becky Early], Alan Powers (Conran Octopus, 1999)
Rachael Howard (The Gallery, 1998) – A catalogue of some of Howard's work, including lots of images of the Swimmers ties, her sketches and other textiles.
Techno Textiles [Becky Early], Sarah Braddock (Thames and Hudson, 1998)
Yinka Shonibare: Be-Muse, C. Perella and E. di Majo (Ministero Attivita Cultural, 2002)

INDEX